Water All Around the Earth

Ann Weil

Contents

Rigby

A Harcourt Achieve Imprint

www.Rigby.com
1-800-531-5015

1 A Planet of Water

Think of the many different ways we use water every day. We drink it, wash with it, cook with it, play in it, and brush our teeth with it. We turn a faucet, and out it comes. But where exactly is our water coming from?

Many people use water to wash their cars or vans.

Large reservoirs like this one can supply enough water for everyone in a city to use.

Most people in the United States get their water from public water supplies that use rivers, lakes, wells, and **reservoirs.** A reservoir is a place where water is collected and stored for later use. Thanks to all of these sources of water, even people in some of the driest parts of the world get the water they need.

How Much Water Is There?

How much water do you think there is on and around our planet? The answer may be more than you might guess. Water covers between 70 and 75 percent of Earth's surface and there's a lot more water underground. There's even water in the air.

Earth looks blue from outer space because most of its surface is covered with water.

Milk jugs hold 1 gallon of liquid. The huge swimming pool used at the Olympic Games holds 1 million gallons of liquid. A section of ocean 1 mile deep, 1 mile long, and 1 mile wide—a cubic mile—can hold as much liquid as 1 million Olympic swimming pools put together. And the total water supply of the world is about 330 million cubic miles. That's a lot of water!

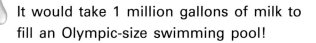
It would take 1 million gallons of milk to fill an Olympic-size swimming pool!

Water on Earth

Most of the water on Earth is ocean water. The water in oceans, seas, rivers, streams, lakes, and ponds is called **surface water** because it is found on the surface of the earth. When you go swimming or boating, you are using surface water. While the majority of surface water is ocean water, we do not use this water in our homes because it is salty. A lot of the water we use at home every day comes from rivers.

People can sail boats on the oceans of Earth.

Land and Water on Earth

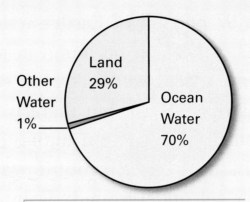

Pie chart:
- Land 29%
- Ocean Water 70%
- Other Water 1%

Only about 29 percent of Earth's surface is covered with land. The rest is water.

Water Underground

Even though 97 percent of Earth's water is found in oceans, water can be found in other places also—some places we can't even see! Surface water is easy to see, but there is more water underground. Water found underneath the surface of Earth is called **ground water.** How does water get underground? Rainwater seeps deep down into the soil until it reaches hard rock and can't go any farther.

There isn't much surface water in the desert. People who live there have to dig wells to get ground water from below the surface of Earth.

People use pipes to bring water from underground aquifers up to the surface. Once this water is collected on the surface, people can use it.

People dig wells to get ground water for their families, and governments put pipes into underground sources of water called **aquifers** to supply cities with water. Ground water is a very important source of fresh water for us. It is the largest single supply of fresh water that we can use.

Water in the Air

Step outside, look up, and what do you see? Is that a cloud? Clouds often look like bunches of cotton balls stuck together, but clouds are really made up of tiny drops of water. There is also **water vapor** in the air that we can't even see.

We breathe water in and out with every breath we take. Have you ever seen your breath make small clouds on a very cold day? What you are seeing is the warm water vapor you are breathing out as it cools down in the cold air.

When the water in your breath touches cold air, it becomes visible!

Even on hot, sunny days when there isn't a cloud in the sky, there is still moisture—or water—in the air. The amount of moisture in the air is called humidity. Some wet places, like tropical rainforests, are very humid, while dry deserts have a very low level of humidity.

Rainforests are the wettest places on Earth and have the highest levels of humidity.

2 Using Water Every Day

Did you brush your teeth this morning? Did you wash your hands before lunch? Did you take a drink from the water fountain after gym class? You have probably been using water all day without even thinking about it. People all over the world use water on Earth, water underground, and water in the air to meet their needs every day.

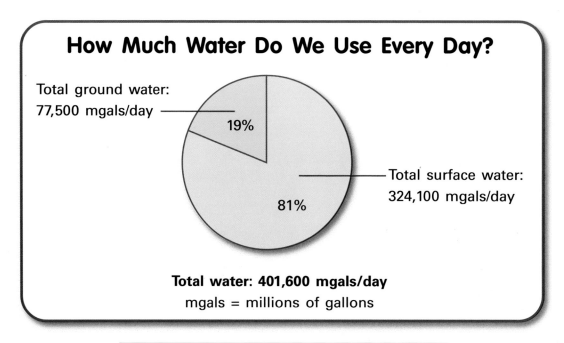

How Much Water Do We Use Every Day?

Total ground water: 77,500 mgals/day

19%

Total surface water: 324,100 mgals/day

81%

Total water: 401,600 mgals/day
mgals = millions of gallons

People in the United States use more than 400,000 million gallons of water every day.

How Water on Earth Is Used

Many people in the United States get their water from rivers or other sources of surface water. Surface water has many different uses, and people all over the world depend on it to wash, drink, cook, and survive.

Surface water is used on farms to grow crops. Industries use surface water from rivers and streams to make many of the products we need, such as paper and metal. We even use surface water to make electricity to light our homes.

Some power plants use waterfalls—another kind of surface water—to make electricity.

How Water Underground Is Used

Ground water is a good source of drinking water and is often easier to use than surface water. Sometimes water from deep underground comes to the surface and forms springs that communities depend on for clean water. In places where surface water is scarce, such as deserts, people can't survive without ground water.

The water that flows in springs comes from deep underground.

Strong metal drills can tunnel through even solid rock to reach underground sources of water. Many people drill wells to get water in the desert.

Many homes are far away from surface water, but ground water may be flowing right underneath their front doors. Sometimes people dig tunnels to ground water in order to make wells. Then ground water can be pumped up into homes and businesses.

How Water in the Air Is Used

What can you do if there's no surface or ground water available in your area? Look up! If you see fog or low clouds, you may have all the water you need.

Chungungo is a small fishing village in Chile. The people living there have no ground water to use, and it almost never rains. However, it is very foggy most of the time, and this fog contains more than enough water to supply the village. A fog catcher was created to change the fog into usable water. Similar fog-catching systems are also operating in other parts of South America, like Peru and Ecuador.

Water from the air forms drops on these fog catchers. People then collect the water for drinking, washing, and growing crops.

The Fog Catcher

1. Water in the air forms drops on the mesh of the fog catcher as the fog passes through it.

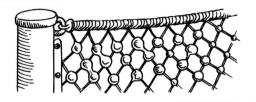

2. Water drips down into gutters that lead to a reservoir.

3. Pipes take the water to where it is needed, into homes for drinking and washing, and into fields to water crops.

4a. People use the water for drinking and washing.

4b. People use the water to grow vegetable gardens.

17

3 Fresh or Salty?

Are you thirsty? Why not try a drink of water from a drinking fountain? Ah, it's so cool and refreshing! That's fresh water. The water in rivers and streams is usually fresh water. A stream or river can start by flowing down from a high mountain lake or rising up from a spring in the ground. All of this fresh water is usable, as long as it doesn't become polluted.

The World's Five Longest Rivers:
- The Nile River, Africa
- The Amazon River, South America
- The Yangtze River, Asia
- The Mississippi River, North America
- The Yenisey-Angara River, Asia

Do you remember that 1 cubic mile can hold as much water as 1 million Olympic swimming pools? There are more than 2 million cubic miles of fresh water in and on Earth, but the biggest source of fresh water isn't usable—it's frozen solid in **glaciers** and ice caps.

Most of the fresh water on Earth is frozen in ice sheets and glaciers.

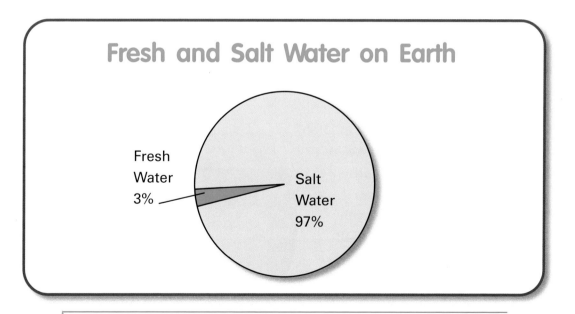

Fresh and Salt Water on Earth

Fresh Water 3%

Salt Water 97%

Most of the water on Earth is salt water found in the oceans.

Salt Water

Most of Earth's water is salt water and is found in the oceans. But there are other, smaller bodies of salt water found inland. So why is some water salty while other water isn't?

As water flows over rocks and underground, tiny bits of minerals from the ground—like salt—dissolve into the water. Even fresh water from streams and rivers contains a small amount of salt, but not enough for it to taste salty. Sometimes this slightly salty water flows into a lake, and then the lake becomes salty.

The Great Salt Lake, in Utah, is the largest salt lake in North America. Nearby plants and rocks are sometimes coated with salt from the Great Salt Lake's waters.

Oceans got some of their salt this way, but there are other reasons the oceans are so salty. Often volcanoes erupt and send minerals into the ocean. There are also places on the ocean floor where seawater can seep into the hot, rocky crust of Earth. The water becomes very hot and dissolves minerals that then flow back up into the rest of the ocean's water.

The minerals that are dissolved in this water have stained the ground many beautiful colors where the water flows.

The lava from this erupting volcano is carrying minerals into the ocean.

4 Water Wonders

If you just know where to look, watching water can be as much fun as playing an exciting video game. Many people travel thousands of miles to see water wonders.

Old Faithful

If you visit Yellowstone National Park, you will want to see Old Faithful erupt. Many times a day, the heat from underground volcanoes warms ground water until it turns to steam, shoots through tunnels of rock, and sprays out high above Earth's surface. Old Faithful is a remarkable **geyser** because we can predict when it will erupt!

Many people visit Yellowstone National Park each year to watch Old Faithful erupt.

Fun Facts About Old Faithful

- Old Faithful erupts about 20 times a day.
- Old Faithful's eruptions last 1.5 to 5 minutes.
- Old Faithful sprays 3,700 to 8,400 gallons of water each time it erupts. A bathtub holds about 50 gallons of water, so this geyser erupts as much water as about 100 bathtubs can hold!

Old Faithful's eruptions are so tall that they even can be seen from very far away. Water shoots from 100 to 180 feet into the air. This is taller than many buildings!

The Dead Sea

The Dead Sea is a large salt lake in Asia, between Israel and Jordan. It is also the lowest water surface on Earth, at about 1,320 feet below sea level.

The water in the Dead Sea is about nine times as salty as the water in the ocean, allowing people to float very high on its surface.

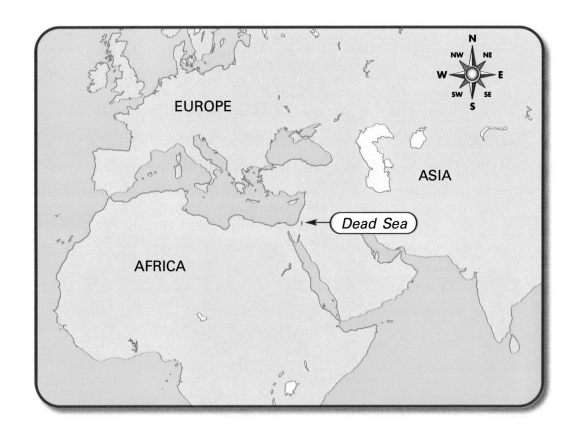

The Dead Sea is the saltiest body of water in the world. All of this salt makes it very easy for swimmers to float in the Dead Sea. However, the salt also makes it very difficult for life to grow there. Few plants and no fish live in these waters, which is why this unusual lake is called the Dead Sea.

Niagara Falls

Millions of tourists from all over the world come to see Niagara Falls every year. Niagara Falls is located between the United States and Canada. People can watch the falls from either side, from a boat ride below the falls, or from behind the curtain of falling water.

People come from many places to look at Niagara Falls. All of the falling water makes a very loud crashing noise as it smashes into the river at the bottom.

Niagara Falls isn't the tallest waterfall in the world, but many people think it is one of the most beautiful. As the water crashes down, it sprays water high into the air, and on sunny days, rainbows appear in the mist.

Water falls 3,212 feet from the top of Angel Falls to the bottom.

Wakulla Springs

Wakulla Springs, in Florida, is one of the largest and deepest freshwater springs in the world. Each minute over 400 gallons of water flow up to the surface from an underground river. Where does all this water come from? That mystery remains hidden deep below Wakulla Springs.

People ride over Wakulla Springs in glass-bottomed boats so that they can look down and see the animals, plants, and rocks below.

Many kinds of animals, like this alligator, live in the clear waters of Wakulla Springs.

The water of Wakulla Springs is very clear and blue.

Wakulla Springs Cave Diving Expeditions

Exploring the Wakulla Springs caves was one of the most challenging underwater trips people had ever taken because of the long distances of the underwater tunnels and the depth of the water—about 300 feet. The water pressure at 300 feet can hurt or even kill a diver. New machines enabled divers to travel over 1 mile into one of the underwater caves, but the source of the spring still remains a mystery.

Río Camuy

Río Camuy, in Puerto Rico, may be one of the biggest underground river systems in the western part of the world with miles of caves that tourists can explore. Getting into the caves is an adventure—many groups are lowered down by ropes—but it's definitely worth the trip. Inside the caves, there are stunning natural rock formations that look like giant faces and animals, as well as paintings and carvings created by the Taíno people who lived about 500 years ago. You can also see seashells and fossils stuck into the rock of the caves. They are left over from when this area was an ancient coral reef. Like the Dead Sea, Niagara Falls, and Wakulla Springs, Río Camuy offers us an exciting look at a great treasure: the water all around Earth!

Rock formations exist deep inside the caves of Río Camuy.

People who lived hundreds of years ago painted this interesting face on the wall of this cave.

Water inside the caves helps to grow lush jungle plants that hikers like to visit.

Glossary

aquifer a layer of underground rock or soil that contains water

geyser a spring that sprays a fountain of hot water and steam into the air

glacier a large piece of ice that moves or spreads slowly over Earth

ground water water found underneath the surface of Earth

reservoir a place where people collect and store water to be used later

surface water water found on the surface of Earth

water vapor water that is present in the air as a gas

Index